Animal Lives

SNAKES

Sally Morgan

QEB Publishing

Library of Congress Control Number:
2005921285

ISBN 1-59566-121-2

Written by Sally Morgan
Designed by Q2A Solutions
Editor Tom Jackson
Map by PCGraphics (UK) Ltd

Publisher Steve Evans
Creative Director Louise Morley
Editorial Manager Jean Coppendale

Printed and bound in China

Picture Credits

Getty: Front cover, James Martin 4, Tim Davis
5, Anthony Bannister 11, Paul Chesley 15
Corbis: Anthony Bannister 5, Joe McDonald
6, David A. Northcott 7, 12, 19 Tony Hamblin
10, Chris Mattison 11, Nigel J. Denis 15,
Rod Patterson 22–23, Patricia Fogden 23,
Chris Newton 25, Charles Philip Cangialosi
25, David Bartruff 29, George McCarthy 30
Stillpictures: Sylvian Cordier 13, 30,
James Gerholdt 16, 19, Matt Meadows 17,
Gunter Ziesler 21, Martin Harvey 23,
Daniel Heuclin 24, BIOS 26, Roland Seitre 27,
Theirry Thomas 28–29, Kelvin Aitken 28,
Hans Pfletschinger 30
Ecoscene: Dennis Johnson 8–9
NHPA: Martin Wendler 20

Words in **bold** are
explained in the
Glossary on page 31.

Contents

Snakes

Snakes belong to a group of animals called **reptiles**. Reptiles are animals that have scaly skin. Other reptiles include lizards, crocodiles, and turtles.

Cobras are dangerous snakes. When they feel threatened, they raise their heads and hiss at their attacker.

Most reptiles have four legs and a long tail. But snakes don't have legs; instead they have a very long backbone. This allows them to bend in any direction and even tie themselves into coils and knots.

snake fact

A python's backbone is made up of 500 separate bones. You have only 206 bones in your whole body.

Sea snakes have flattened tails that they use as paddles.

Most snakes live on land. They burrow into sand and under rocks, and others live in the branches of trees. In some warm parts of the world, snakes swim in water. Snakes, such as the olive sea snake, live out at sea all the time and never see dry land.

Vinesnakes grow up to 5 feet (1.5 m) long and are very thin. They live in trees where it is difficult for enemies to see them.

Snake types

There are almost 3,000 species, or types, of snake. They range in size from small garter snakes that are only 5 inches (12 cm) long, to the gigantic boas and pythons, which are more than 30 feet (10 m) long. Most snakes are between 10 inches (25 cm) and 5 feet (1.5 m) in length.

snake

The tentacle snake is named after the pair of fleshy tentacles on either side of its mouth. These are not seen on any other type of snake.

fact

Garter snakes are found in North America. They live close to water.

Snake colors

Many snakes have dull colors, with brown, gray, and black skin. These colors blend in well with the colors on the ground. Tree snakes are often green, so they can hide among the leaves.

However, some snakes have red and yellow **scales**. These bright colors are a warning that the snake is **poisonous**.

The emerald tree boa is a bright green snake that lies in wait for its prey, coiled around branches in trees.

7

Where do you find snakes?

Snakes are mostly found in the warmer parts of the world. They do not live near the North and South Poles, where it is far too cold for them. Many islands, including Iceland, Ireland, and New Zealand, do not have any snakes living on them either. Sea snakes are found in the warmer seas in the world.

These adders are basking in the early morning sun to warm up

North America

Europe

Asia

Atlantic
Ocean

Africa

Pacific
Ocean

Pacific
Ocean

South
America

Indian
Ocean

Australia

Antarctic Ocean

Antarctica

Areas where land snakes are found
Areas where sea snakes are found

Looking for heat

Snakes prefer warm places because they are **ectothermic** animals. This means they take heat from their surroundings, and their body temperature is the same temperature as their environment. When the temperature around a snake falls, so does its body temperature.

Snakes bask in the morning sun to warm up after a cold night. They can't survive in cold places because their bodies would never get warm enough. Snakes that do live in chilly parts of the world stay in a warm hole all winter.

snake

Every spring throughout North America, thousands of garter snakes emerge together from their underground winter shelters.

fact

Beginning life

Snake

The reticulated and Burmese pythons produce the most eggs, laying clutches of up to 100 eggs.

fact

Most snakes lay eggs. Snake eggs are leathery and do not have a hard shell like a bird's egg. Female snakes lay their eggs in a sheltered spot and leave without waiting for the eggs to hatch. A few species, like pythons, watch over their eggs. It takes a few weeks for the baby snake to develop inside the egg. When it is time to hatch, the baby snake chips its way out using a special egg tooth.

The female snake lays her eggs in a nest.

The young snake is coiled up inside the egg. When it hatches, it is seven times longer than the egg.

Live bearers

Some snakes do not lay eggs; instead, the eggs develop inside the mother's body. The young snakes hatch out from the eggs while they are still inside their mother. The mother then gives birth to them. These snakes are called live bearers.

The female eyelash viper gives birth to live young that are small versions of the adult snakes.

Growing up

Newly hatched snakes look like minature versions of the adults. Their parents do not look after them, so the young snakes have to move to a safe place and find food by themselves.

The baby snakes quickly slither away from the nest before they are spotted by **predators**.

Molting

A snake's scaly skin is tough and does not stretch. As a snake grows, its skin gets tight. Young snakes must **molt**, or shed their skins, to grow bigger.

When they are ready to molt, an oil spreads under the outer layer of skin. The old skin splits and slips off in one piece, leaving a shiny new skin underneath.

Snakes never stop growing. They molt whenever they grow too big for their skin.

snake

Snakes do not have eyelids to protect their eyes. Instead they have a see-through scale covering each eye.

fact

Slithering

Snakes do not have legs like lizards and other reptiles. They move in a completely different way—they slither along the ground.

The body of this rattlesnake forms a series of curves as it winds across the ground.

Tree snakes, such as this boomslang, have long, thin bodies. They spread their weight across many branches.

Wiggling and gliding

Most wiggle across the ground, moving from side to side. The snake's body follows its head in a series of curves. Heavy snakes and those that creep up on their **prey**, glide slowly forward in a straight line. The scales underneath their body hook onto the ground, pulling the snake forward.

14

Sidewinding

It is difficult for a snake to slither across sand because it is too loose to push against. Snakes that live in deserts, such as sidewinders, have found the answer—they move sideways.

Sidewinders throw their head sideways while the rest of their body stays on the ground. Once their head is back on the ground, the rest of the body follows the head sideways, creating a curling movement.

snake

Snakes can't slither very quickly. Even the fastest moving snakes, the African mambas, only travel at 6½ mph (11 km per hour) over a short distance.

fact

The tracks of the sidewinder show that not all of its body touches the ground at the same time.

15

Snake senses

Snakes use their senses to find their way around and to catch prey. Snakes can't see very well, but they have excellent hearing and a very good sense of smell. Their ears are completely covered but can pick up **vibrations** in the ground. These vibrations tell them if an animal is moving nearby.

Snakes flick out their forked tongue through a slot in their upper jaw.

Forked tongues

Snakes taste the air with their forked tongue. When a snake flicks its tongue out of its mouth, the tongue picks up scent particles from the air. The tongue's forks are then pushed into a special sense organ on the roof of the snake's mouth.

Hunting at night

Pit vipers and pythons hunt at night. They can't see much in the dark, but they can detect the heat given off by the bodies of their prey. Snakes do this using heat-sensitive pits on their face.

Pit vipers can detect heat with the pits on their snout.

17

Predators

Snakes are **predators**, which means they kill other animals for food. Many snakes hunt a range of animals, from insects and worms to lizards and mice. Others hunt only one kind of animal. For example, hook-nosed snakes eat only spiders.

It is not just small animals that get eaten by snakes. Big animals, like deer, goats, and even people, get swallowed up by snakes like giant boa constrictors and pythons.

The Gabon viper's color and pattern helps it hide among fallen leaves while it waits to ambush prey.

Swallowing prey

Snakes do not have any feet, so they can't hold their food and bite chunks out of it. Instead, snakes swallow their prey in one piece, usually head first.

Snakes can open their mouth very wide, because their lower jaw is loosely joined to the bottom of their skull. This means even large animals can fit through.

snake

The common egg-eater snake swallows bird eggs that are up to four times the size of its head. That's like a person swallowing a car tire.

fact

Snakes have backward facing teeth to stop their prey from escaping.

Constrictors

Many of the largest snakes, such as the boas and pythons, are constrictors. These snakes squeeze, or constrict, their prey to death.

Tighter and tighter

Once a constrictor has trapped its prey, it coils its body around its victim. The coils get tighter and tighter. As the prey breathes out, the snake tightens the coils. Eventually the victim can't breathe or pump blood around its body.

snake

The world's largest snake, the green anaconda of South America, is powerful enough to kill caimans. This giant snake ambushes its prey in the water.

fact

This anaconda has caught a caiman, a type of crocodile, in the Amazon jungle.

Swallowed whole

Once the prey is dead, the snake relaxes and uncoils slightly, and begins to swallow its victim head first.

The snake's skin is very elastic and it stretches to make room for a large meal. This makes a bulge in the snake's body, which gradually moves along the body, getting smaller as it is digested. Many snakes don't eat regular meals. The largest snakes can survive on one good meal a year.

The constrictor wraps itself around its prey so the animal can't escape.

21

Poisonous snakes

Many snakes produce **venom.** They do this to kill their prey and to protect themselves if they are threatened.

The most poisonous snakes are the vipers, cobras, sea snakes, and the Australian brown snakes. They use their venom to kill prey and fight off attackers.

snake

One of the most poisonous snakes is the Australian inland taipan. The venom in one bite is enough to kill 200,000 mice!

fact

Spitting cobras spit venom into the eyes of their prey to blind them.

Fangs

A snake's venom is produced in a gland in its head and is pumped into its prey through a long, sharp tooth, called a fang. When the snake bites, the venom flows along the fang into the prey. Some venom kills quickly, other venom just weakens the prey.

Some venom may start to break down the skin around the bite. The venom of the western diamond-backed rattlesnakes does this.

This sedge viper is ready to attack. Its fangs are on its upper jaw.

The red, yellow, and black stripes of this coral snake warn other animals that it is very poisonous.

23

Snake defenses

Snakes may be predators, but are themselves often hunted by other animals; for example, mongooses and secretary birds are expert snake killers. They can even kill a snake that has deadly venom.

snake

The rubber boa's head and tail are difficult to tell apart. When threatened, the snake rolls into a ball and waves its tail, pretending its tail is its head.

fact

Camouflage

Venomous snakes can fight back when attacked, but nonpoisonous snakes have other ways of protecting themselves. Most snakes are well **camouflaged** and they lie still so predators can't spot them easily.

The mongoose attacks and kills poisonous snakes, such as this cobra.

Copy cats

Several nonvenomous snakes pretend to be poisonous by looking very similar to a venomous species. The bright colors put off a predator, who thinks it might get bitten.

The harmless milk snake is often mistaken for the poisonous coral snake.

When threatened, the grass snake pretends to be dead.

Snakes and people

Many people are scared of snakes even though most snakes are harmless. People think that snakes are cold, slimy animals, but they are warm and dry to the touch.

Death from snake bite

Only a few snakes will attack a person; most will just slither away. But if the snake feels threatened, it will strike back. In places where there are many dangerous snakes, such as India, people often get bitten. There are medicines that stop the venom from working. However, if a person who has been bitten does not get treatment quickly, they may die.

A rattlesnake has a rattle on its tail, which is used to scare away attackers. The rattle is made up of sections of dried skin that knock together

snake & fact

As many as 100,000 people die each year from snake bites, mostly in country areas of Africa and India.

To milk a snake, its fangs are pushed against a hard surface. This makes the venom ooze out.

Useful venom

Scientists are using some snake venom to make medicines; for example, one venom is used to reduce high blood pressure. The venom is removed from the snake in a process called **milking**.

27

Snakes under threat

Many snakes are under threat, and some species may even become **extinct**.

Habitat loss

The main reason why many snakes are dying out is because their **habitats** are being destroyed. The forests and meadows where snakes are found are being turned into farms and towns.

Snakes that live in tropical rain forests can't survive anywhere else once the forest is cleared.

28

Hunted

Often snakes are killed because they are poisonous. For example, rattlesnakes are sometimes killed in huge numbers in the United States. Other snakes are killed for their skin, which is used to make handbags, shoes, and souvenirs. The beautiful but deadly sea krait is especially rare because of this.

Snake skin is soft and the scales make an attractive pattern.

Conserving snakes

It is very important that habitats are saved to protect endangered snakes. Many species that are under threat of extinction are bred in zoos. They may be released into the wild in the future.

Thousands of sea kraits are caught each year for their skin.

Life cycle

The female snake lays a **clutch** of eggs on the ground. Tiny snakes, that look like miniature adults, hatch after one to three months. The young snakes grow quickly and shed their skin regularly. Most snakes live for about ten years, but some live as long as forty years in zoos.

Baby snake hatching out of an egg.

Molting

Fully grown snake

Glossary

camouflage coloring that blends in with the background

clutch a group of eggs laid at the same time

ectothermic when an animal's body temperature is the same temperature as its surroundings; scientists call this ectothermy

extinct when a species or type of animal has died out

habitat the place where an animal or plant lives

milking the name given to the process of collecting snake venom

molt to shed skin, feathers, or hair

poison a very harmful substance that stops the body from working properly

predator an animal that hunts other animals

prey an animal that is hunted by another animal

reptile an animal that is covered in hard scales and lays leathery eggs

scales thin flakes that form the skin of a reptile

venom poison produced by many snakes to kill their prey and to protect themselves

vibrations a slight movement, shake, or tremble

Index